GIFTED & TALENTED®

*To develop
your child's gifts
and talents*

PUZZLES & GAMES

FOR READING & MATH

GIFTED
&
TALENTED®

*To develop
your child's gifts
and talents*

PUZZLES & GAMES

FOR READING & MATH

A Workbook for Ages 6–8

Written by Nancy Casolaro and Kaye Furlong
Illustrated by Leesa Whitten

Lowell House House
Juvenile
Los Angeles
CONTEMPORARY
BOOKS
Chicago

Manufactured in the United States of America

ISBN 1-56565-065-4

10 9 8 7 6 5 4 3

Cover design: Brenda Leach
Cover illustration: Kerry Manwaring

GIFTED AND TALENTED WORKBOOKS will help develop your child's natural talents and gifts by providing activities to enhance critical and creative thinking skills. These skills of logic and reasoning teach children **how** to think. They are precisely the skills emphasized by teachers of gifted and talented children.

Thinking skills are the skills needed to be able to learn anything at any time. Unlike events, words, and teaching methods, thinking skills never change. If a child has a grasp of how to think, school success and even success in life will become more assured. In addition, the child will become self-confident as he or she approaches new tasks with the ability to think them through and discover solutions.

GIFTED AND TALENTED WORKBOOKS present these skills in a unique way, combining the basic subject areas of reading, language arts, and math with thinking skills. The top of each page is labeled to indicate the specific thinking skill developed. Here are some of the skills you will find:

- Deduction – the ability to reach a logical conclusion by interpreting clues

- Understanding relationships – the ability to recognize how objects, shapes, and words are similar or dissimilar; to classify and categorize

- Sequencing – the ability to organize events, numbers; to recognize patterns

- Inference – the ability to reach logical conclusions from given or assumed evidence

- Creative thinking – the ability to generate unique ideas; to compare and contrast the same elements in different situations; to present imaginative solutions to problems

How to Use Gifted & Talented Workbooks

Each book contains activities that challenge children. The activities vary in range from easier to more difficult. You may need to work with your child on many of the pages, especially with the child who is a non-reader. However, even a non-reader can master thinking skills, and the sooner your child learns how to think, the better. Read the directions to your child, and if necessary, explain them. Let your child choose to do the activities that interest him or her. When interest wanes, stop. A page or two at a time may be enough, as the child should have fun while learning.

It is important to remember that these activities are designed to teach your child **how to think,** not how to find the right answer. Teachers of gifted children are never surprised when a child discovers a new "right" answer. For example, a child may be asked to choose the object that doesn't belong in this group: a table, a chair, a book, a desk. The best answer is **book,** since all the others are furniture. But a child could respond that all of them belong because they all could be found in an office. The best way to react to this type of response is to praise the child and gently point out that there is another answer too. While creativity should be encouraged, your child must look for the best and most **suitable** answer.

GIFTED AND TALENTED WORKBOOKS have been written and designed by teachers. Educationally sound and endorsed by leaders in the gifted field, this series will benefit any child who demonstrates curiosity, imagination, a sense of fun and wonder about the world, and a desire to learn. These books will open your child's mind to new experiences and help fulfill his or her true potential.

Legend says that a magic square brings good luck. A magic square is a square where all sides have the same sum. Use the numbers 1, 2, 3, 4, 5, 6 to make this into a magic square.

Hint: The sum of each side is 15.
　　　The sum of the diagonals is also 15.

Try this game with a friend.

Game Play: Players take turns.

A player may cross off either 1, 2, or 3 ships in the **same** row on each turn.

The player who crosses off the last ship loses.

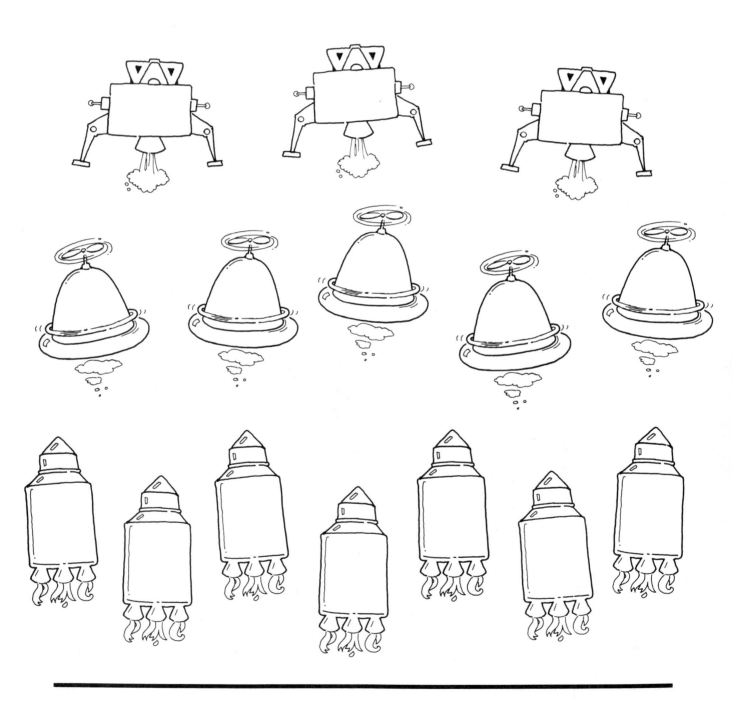

The Fronians are trying to return to the planet Fronia. In order to break through the power shield, they must collect 10 points.

Can you find the way to Fronia by following the arrows?

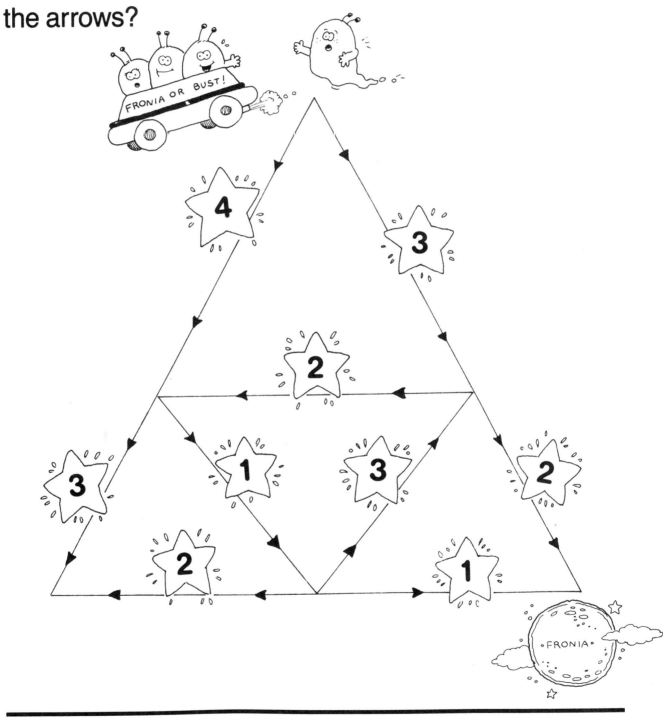

Help the witch complete her spell.

Circle the numbers inside each kettle whose sum is the same as the number on top of the kettle.

The first one is done for you.

Rule: The numbers must be next to, above, or below each other.

YELLOW KETTLE

7	2	3	1	6
4	3	4	2	5
5	6	1	0	5
7	3	4	1	4

RED KETTLE

1	2	5	4
5	6	2	1
1	3	4	2
8	0	5	4

ORANGE KETTLE

6	1	2	8
3	7	3	5
6	7	0	3
4	3	5	8

Try this game of tic-tac-toe.

Instead of using X or O, players choose either the odd numbers 1, 3, 5, 7, 9 or the even numbers 2, 4, 6, 8, 10.

The object of the game is to be the first person to make a row (up and down, across or diagonally) whose sum is 13. Hint: You can use the same number more than once.

Play this game with a friend.

The object of the game is to win the most squares.

Game Play: Make a 4-by-4 dot grid as shown below.

Players take turns drawing a line between two dots. Lines must be up and down or across.

The first player to close a square (see picture) puts his or her initial in the square.

The game continues until there is no place left to move.

The player with the most squares wins.

Help Heather get to the carnival.

Start where Heather is and go through the boxes until you reach the carnival.

Find the path that equals 10.
Find the path that equals 14.
Find the path that equals 19.*
Find the path that equals 22.**

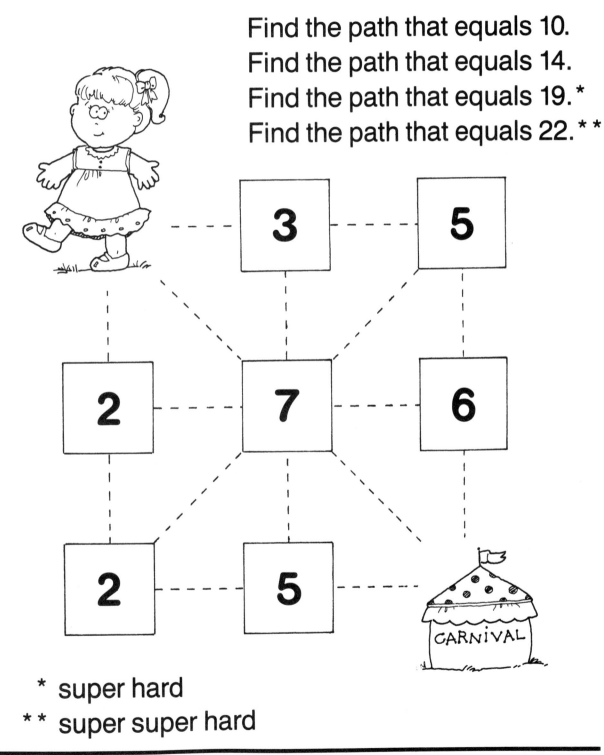

* super hard
** super super hard

The king's pie is filled with blackbirds numbered from 1 to 20.

Can you find which numbers are missing?

_____ and _____.

Which numbers are used more than once?

_____ _____ _____

Which number is greater than 20? _____

Help Katie find the toys in this shop.

Be sure to start where it says START. The first one has been done for you.

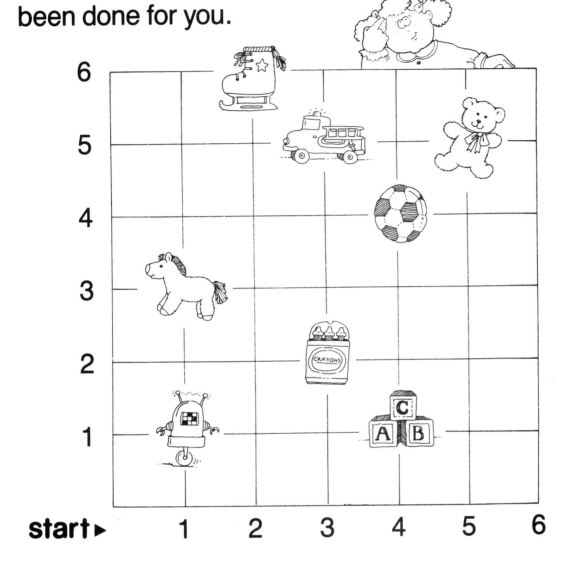

start ▶

	over ▶	up ▲
🖍	3	2
🤖		
🧸		
⛸		

	over ▶	up ▲
⚽		
🚒		
🐴		
ABC		

At Jon's birthday party everyone played video games, but they forgot to put their names on the score cards. Can you write the correct name on each score card? Be sure to read the clues at the bottom of the page.

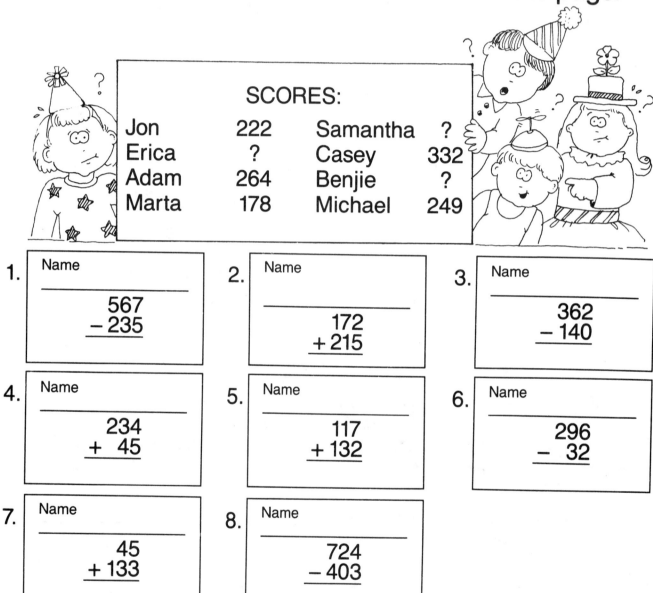

SCORES:

Jon	222	Samantha	?
Erica	?	Casey	332
Adam	264	Benjie	?
Marta	178	Michael	249

1. Name
_____
```
   567
 - 235
```

2. Name
_____
```
   172
 + 215
```

3. Name
_____
```
   362
 - 140
```

4. Name
_____
```
   234
 +  45
```

5. Name
_____
```
   117
 + 132
```

6. Name
_____
```
   296
 -  32
```

7. Name
_____
```
    45
 + 133
```

8. Name
_____
```
   724
 - 403
```

Samantha's score was the highest.

The sum of the numbers in Erica's score is 6.

Benjie's score was higher than Adam's.

16

Help Jana solve this puzzle.

Put a box around the numbers that make 10.
Put a circle around the numbers that make 7.
The numbers must be next to each other or
above and below each other like this:

⎛5⎞		┌3 7┐
⎝2⎠		└1 2┘

5   8   2   6   4

2   1   9   3   4

7   6   3   8   4

3   5   5   2   3

Hint: It's okay if a number is
      in both a box and a circle.

Score: 3 circles   4 boxes   = GREAT!

         4 circles   5 boxes   = SUPER!

         5 circles   6 boxes   = FANTASTIC!

Erica is trying to find out how much her name is worth. Can you help? Look at the chart below to see how much each letter is worth.

E   R   I   C   A
<u>4¢</u> __   __   __   __

Write your name. How much is it worth?

_____

— — — — — — — — — — — — — — ¢

Write 2 friends' names. What are they worth?

_____

— — — — — — — — — — — — — — ¢

_____

— — — — — — — — — — — — — — ¢

Try this with a friend. See who can write the most expensive sentence.

A	B	C	D	E	F	G	H	I	J	K	L	M
2¢	1¢	3¢	1¢	4¢	2¢	3¢	5¢	2¢	3¢	1¢	4¢	5¢

N	O	P	Q	R	S	T	U	V	W	X	Y	Z
2¢	1¢	2¢	3¢	4¢	1¢	5¢	2¢	3¢	1¢	4¢	3¢	5¢

Use this code to solve the puzzle:

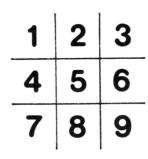

$$\boxed{1} + \boxed{6} =$$

$$\boxed{} + \boxed{} =$$

$$\boxed{9} - \boxed{5} =$$

$$\boxed{} - \boxed{} =$$

$$\boxed{} + \boxed{} =$$

$$\boxed{} + \boxed{} =$$

$$\boxed{} - \boxed{} =$$

$$\boxed{} + \boxed{} =$$

Make some puzzles for a friend.

___ + ___ = ___

___ - ___ = ___

Little Red Riding Hood is going to visit her grandmother. Color the road she should take to get there. Be sure she does not go down the road that equals 6, because the Big Bad Wolf is hiding there.

The road that equals 8 is the fastest way there.

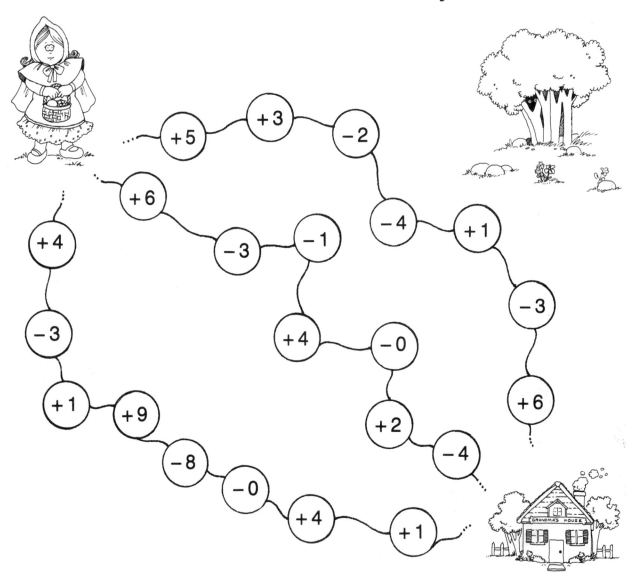

Did you take the fastest road? _____

Can you solve the Tigers' baseball puzzle?

Place all the objects below in the squares.

Rule: Only one of each object may
        be in each row, column, or diagonal.

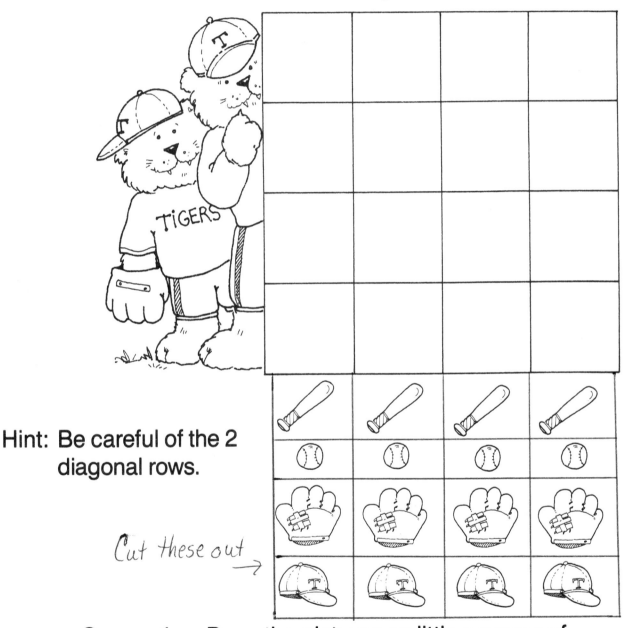

Hint: Be careful of the 2
      diagonal rows.

Cut these out →

Suggestion: Draw the pictures on little squares of
paper so that you can move them around until you
solve the puzzle.

A tangram is an old Chinese puzzle. There are hundreds of pictures that can be made with a tangram.

Cut out the 7 pieces and try the puzzles on the next 3 pages.

Can you make this picture using all 7 tangram pieces?

Hint: You need to turn the ⬦ upside down.

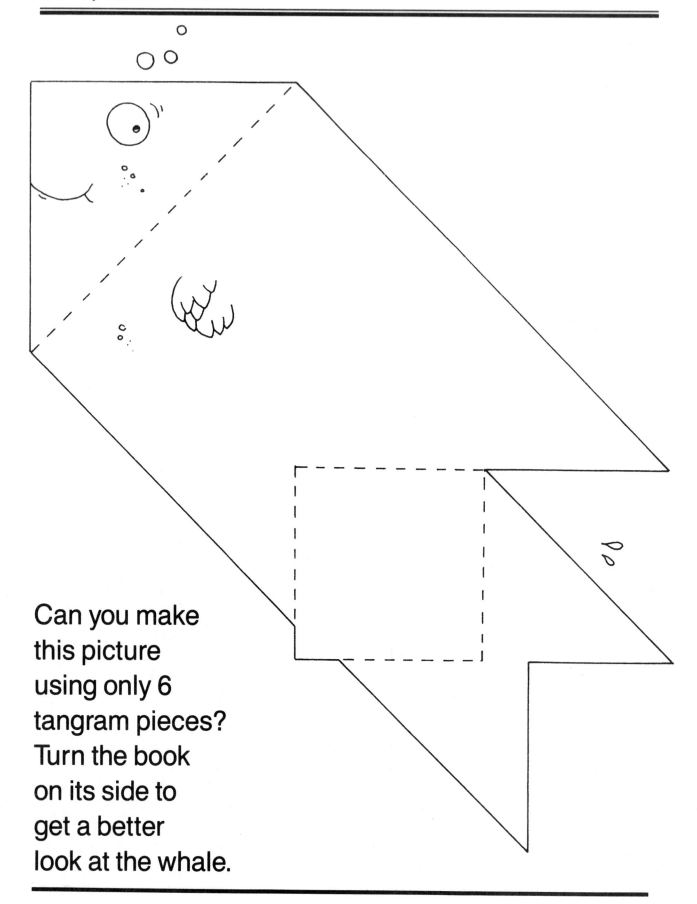

Can you make
this picture
using only 6
tangram pieces?
Turn the book
on its side to
get a better
look at the whale.

Try these puzzles with your tangram.

Can you make a boat?

Pick an animal and try to make it.

Hint: Many people have made cats or ducks.

Try making some numbers or letters.

Can you make a chair?

Make a design for a friend to try.

Help Jason with this puzzle.

Look at the pieces below to find the right answer.

In the town of Backwards, people play tic-tac-toe differently. The winner is the person who does **not** put 3 marks in a column, row, or diagonal.

Can you play by the same rules as the people in Backwards?

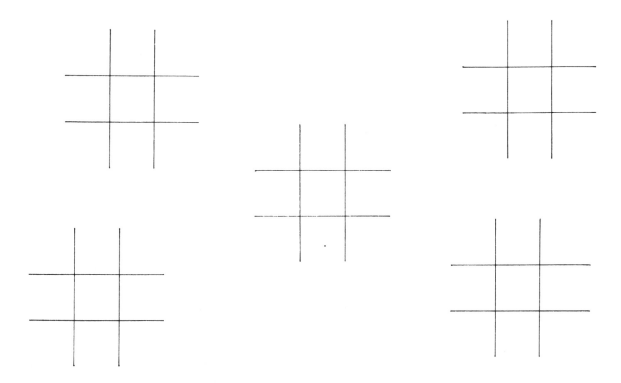

Dara needs a score of 17 to win this video game. What is the greatest amount of objects she can capture to win? _____ Put a red box around these. What is the smallest amount of objects she can capture? _____ Put a blue ring around these.

Help these animals.

Fill in the missing numbers.

Rules: The sum of *each* side must be the same as the number in the animal's mouth.

You can only use the numbers 1, 2, 3, 4, 5, 6, 7, 8, 9.

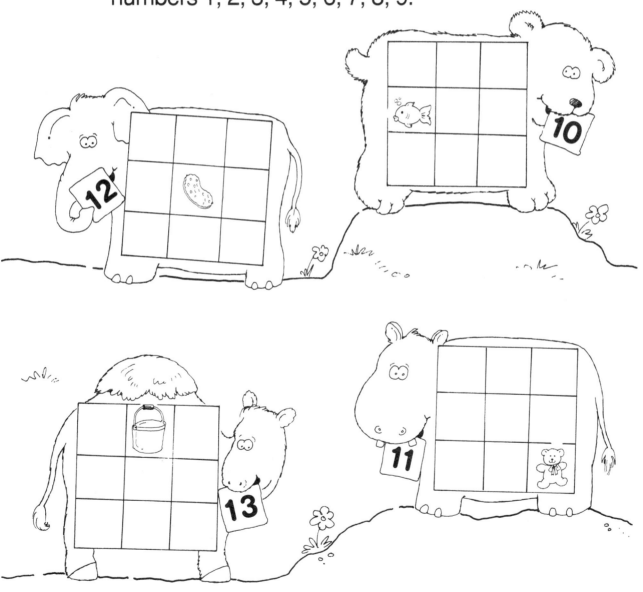

The Gyrosian numbers look different from ours. Here are some numbers from the planet Gyros:

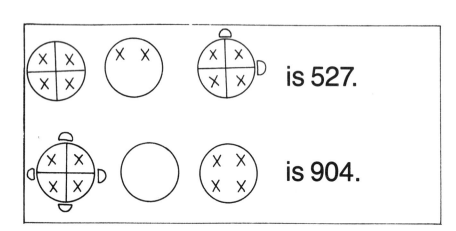

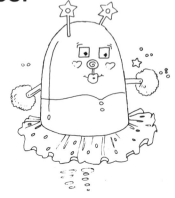

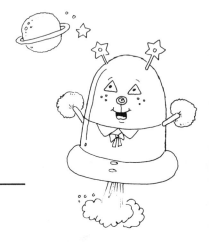

is 527.

is 904.

1. Can you tell what this number is?

_____ _____ _____

2. Can you write the Gyrosian numbers from 0 to 9?

| 0 | 1 | 2 | 3 | 4 |

| 5 | 6 | 7 | 8 | 9 |

Try these problems from Gyros.

Be sure to answer in Gyrosian numbers.

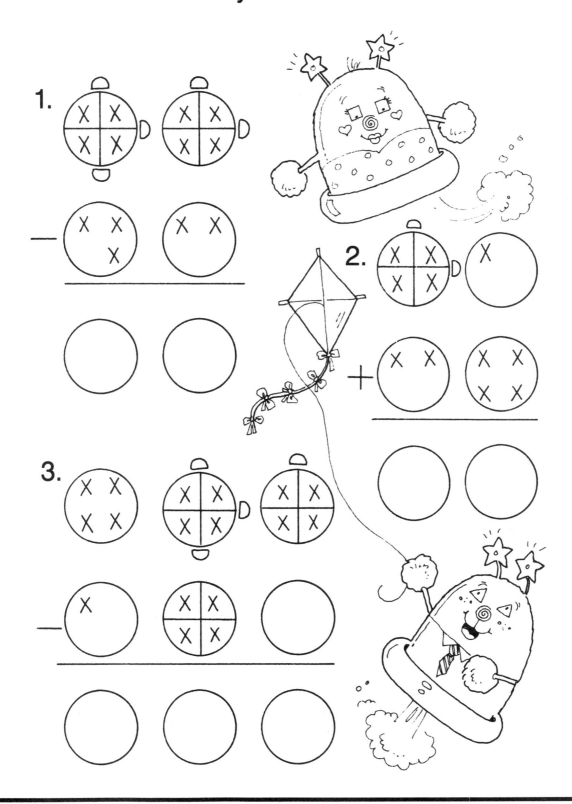

Try this puzzle.

Set 16 toothpicks on a table so they look like the picture on this page.

Can you make 5 squares by moving only 2 toothpicks?

Try this number-search puzzle.

Put a ring around all the numbers that equal 12.
The first one is done for you.

1	3	2	9	5	6
2	6	6	3	4	3
8	4	4	5	7	2
7	2	4	6	5	1

How many did you find?

4 rings = GREAT!

6 rings = SUPER!

9 rings = FANTASTIC!!

Jamie has lost his favorite toy. Help him find it.
Color the numbers *less* than 40 green.
Color the numbers *more* than 40 red.

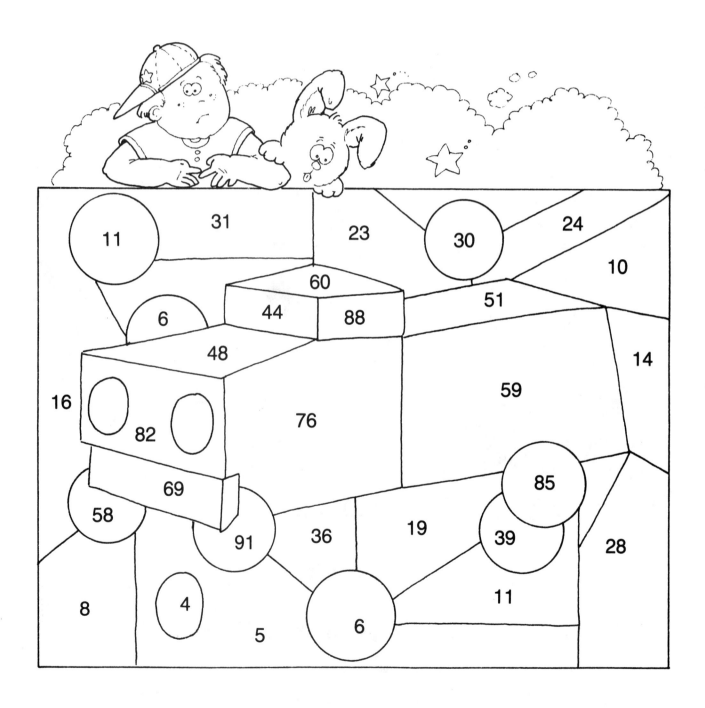

Use the chart below to find out how much this clown is worth.

The clown is worth _____¢.

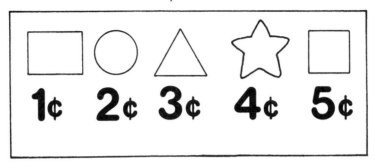

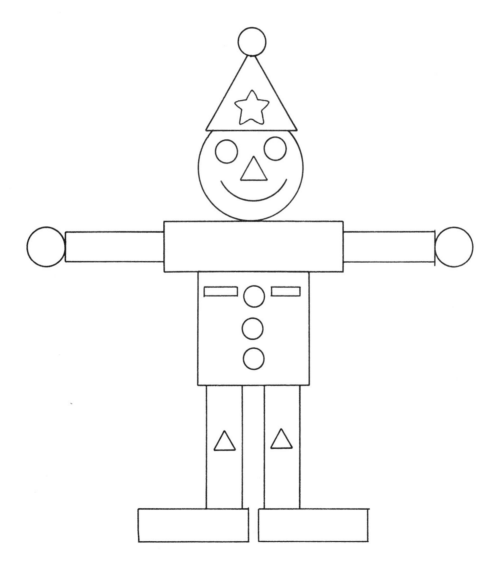

Solve this puzzle.

Use the numbers 4, 5, 6, 7, 8, 9.

Make the sum of the top row = 6.
Make the sum of the middle row = 16.
Make the sum of the bottom row = 17.

Can you color this picture?

Rules: You can only use 4 colors.

No shapes of the same color
can touch each other.

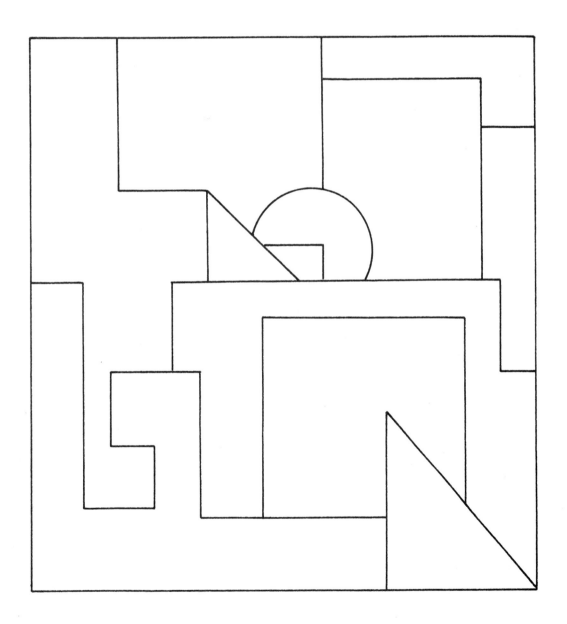

Color the

◯ red

▢ yellow

△ blue

▭ green

How many △ s did you find? _____

Connect the dots to find out what Amanda would like to be when she grows up. Hint: Count by 2s.

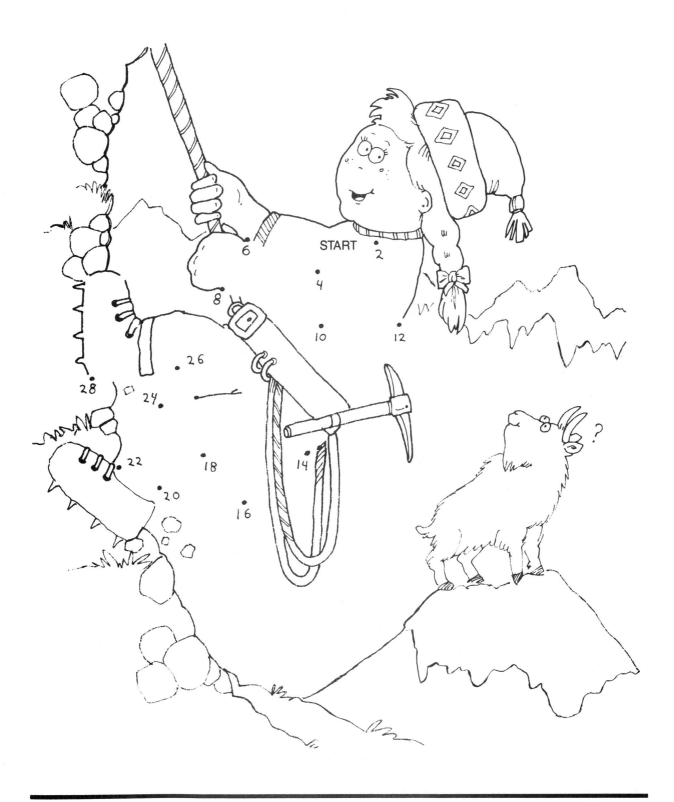

Try these puzzles:

Put 10 pennies on the table just like the circles in this picture. Can you turn the triangle upside down by moving just 3 pennies?

Move these 9 pennies around to make 3 lines with 4 pennies in each line.

Hint: This makes a shape.

Jose is caught in a giant spiderweb. The only way he can break the spider's spell and get out is by finding the path that equals 12. There are two paths that equal 12. The first one is shown. Can you find the other?

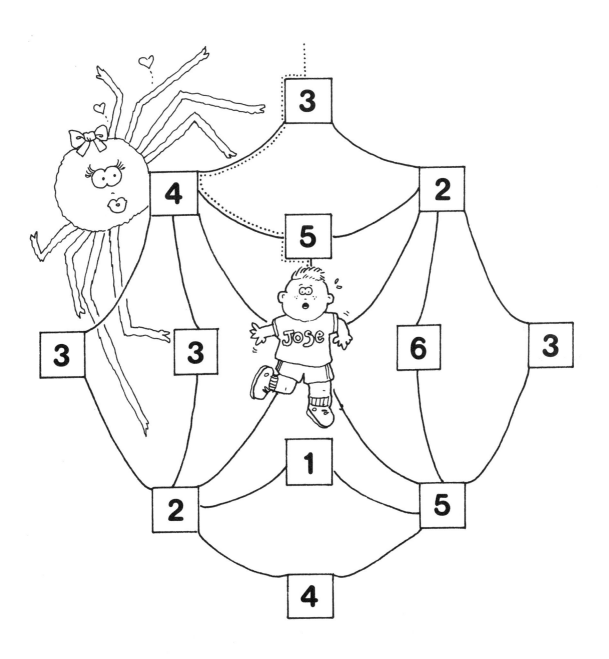

Help Juliana count all the squares in this picture.

_____ squares

Hint: There are more than 10.

How many triangles are in this picture?

_____ triangles

Hint: The triangles are different sizes.

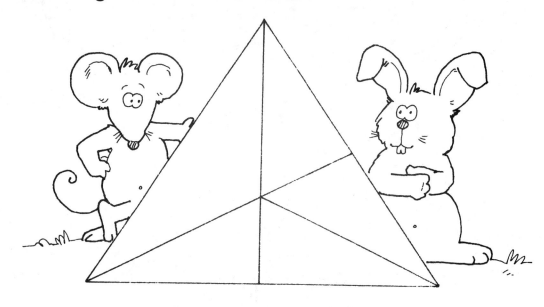

Color all the 7s yellow.
Color all the 8s blue.
Color all the 9s red.

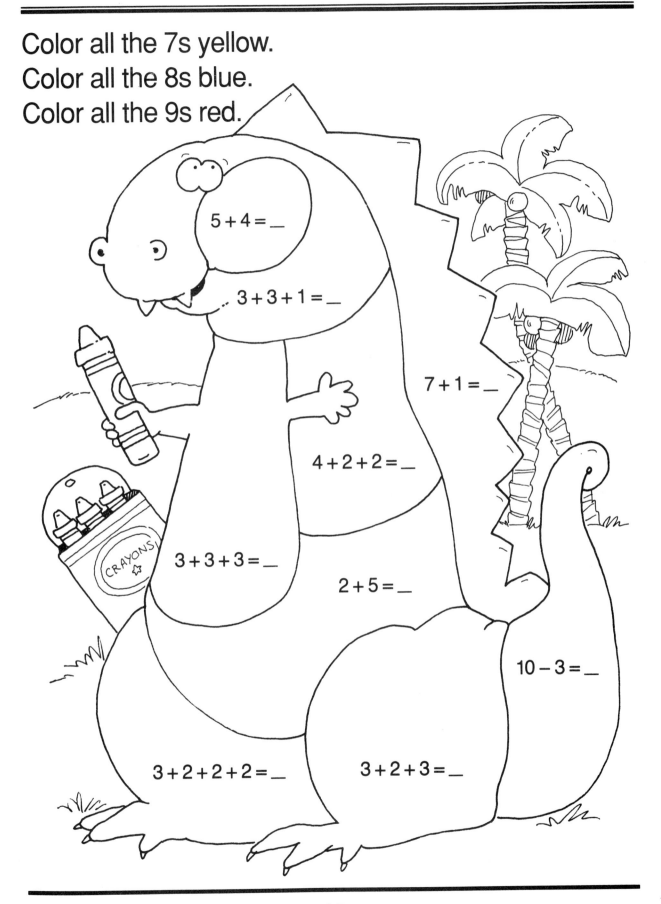

5 + 4 = __

3 + 3 + 1 = __

7 + 1 = __

4 + 2 + 2 = __

3 + 3 + 3 = __

2 + 5 = __

10 − 3 = __

3 + 2 + 2 + 2 = __

3 + 2 + 3 = __

Help this fleet of spaceships get ready for its mission. Number the ships 1, 2, 3, 4, 5, 6, 7, 8.

Rule: Numbers that come before or after each other may not be placed next to one another in *any* direction (even on a diagonal).

Hint: You might want to try this with slips of paper numbered 1 to 8. It will be easier to move them around that way.

Play this game with a friend.

The object of the game is to score the most points.

Game Play: Make a 4-by-4 grid as shown.

		1	
5			
6			7
4	3	2	8

SCORE

even   odd
  8   0

One player chooses odd numbers; the other player chooses even numbers.

The odd number player begins by placing a 1 anywhere on the board.

The next player must put a 2 in the same row either up and down or across.

Rule: No other numbers can come between the two numbers when they are placed. Blank spaces are okay, but another number in between is against the rules.

The player who is able to make the last move wins and scores that number of points (see picture).

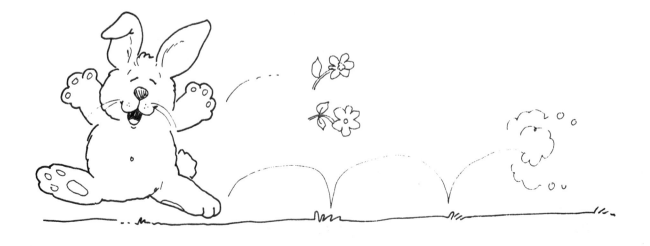

Can you solve this puzzle?

Read the clues and fill in the blanks.

ACROSS

2. There are ___
   minutes in an hour.

4. There are ___
   pennies in a quarter.

5. There are ___ toes
   on three human feet.

7. In 1987 Heather
   had her 6th birthday.
   In what year was she born?

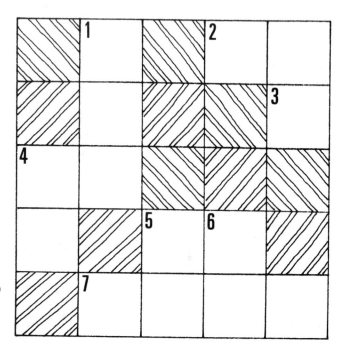

DOWN

1. There are ___ days in a year.

3. There are ___ wheels on a tricycle.

4. There are ___ letters in the alphabet.

5. $16 + 3 =$ ___

6. The number after 57 is ___ .

Can you do this puzzle?

Read the clues and fill in the blanks.

ACROSS

1. $5 + 6 =$ ___

3. The number before 62.

5. The total number of your fingers and toes.

6. An even number less than 4 but greater than 0.

9. 5 dimes and 2 pennies = ___ ¢

10.
$$\begin{array}{r} 988 \\ -\,536 \\ \hline \end{array}$$

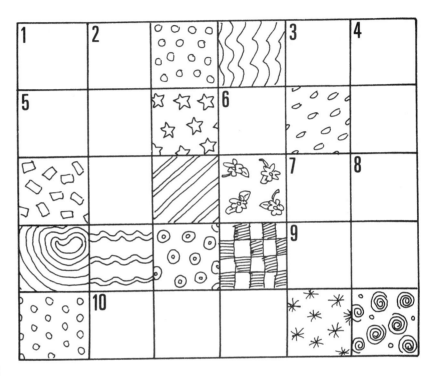

DOWN

1. A dozen cookies is ___ cookies.

2. The number after 99 is ___ .

4.
$$\begin{array}{r} 3743 \\ -\,2311 \\ \hline \end{array}$$

7. The number of fingers on 5 human hands.

8.
$$\begin{array}{r} 20 \\ +\,12 \\ \hline \end{array}$$

Here's a game to play with a friend.

You will need: 1 egg carton

60 beans (peanuts, popcorn kernels, or raisins work well also)

Object of the Game: To collect the most beans.

Game Play: Place 5 beans in each of the slots of the egg carton.

Label one end of the egg carton with your name; the other end with your friend's name.

On your turn, pick up all the beans in one of the slots. Starting with the slot above or below (you must move counterclockwise), place one bean into each slot until you run out of beans. If you pass your end of the carton, you may drop a bean there.

(In the picture the Xs show the beans that were moved on the first turn.)

Continue playing until one side of the egg carton is empty. Count your beans. The player with the most beans wins.

Can you answer this riddle?

What do you get when you cross a cow with a duck?

Color all the boxes with *even* numbers.
Read what is left to find the answer.

4	6	5	1	3	7	2	8	4
I	T	M	I	L	K	C	A	N

3	1	7	6	2	8	4	2	6
A	N	D	W	I	L	L	D	O

4	1	5	7	3	1	5	1	3
I	Q	U	A	C	K	E	R	S

Put the underlined letters together to make a new word.

It starts like

c<u>a</u>r

and ends like

b<u>at</u>

The new word is

_ _ _

It starts like

<u>g</u>o

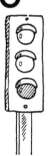

and ends like

n<u>ame</u>

The new word is

_ _ _ _

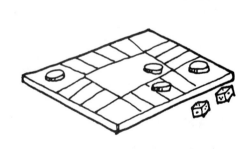

It starts like

<u>b</u>ug

and ends like

t<u>ag</u>

The new word is

_ _ _

Put the underlined letters together to make a new word.

It starts like	and ends like	The new word is
sweets	**r**ing	_ _ _ _ _

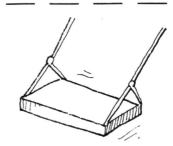

It starts like	and ends like	The new word is
grow	s**een**	_ _ _ _ _

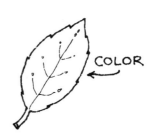

COLOR

It starts like	and ends like	The new word is
chair	r**ain**	_ _ _ _ _

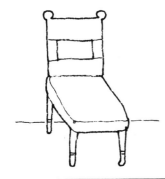

51

1. Put the underlined letters together to make a new word.

2. Color the picture that shows more than one thing.

1. It starts like **br**idge and ends like l**ight**.

It's __ __ __ __ __ __

2. It starts like **sh**ort and ends like t**weet**.

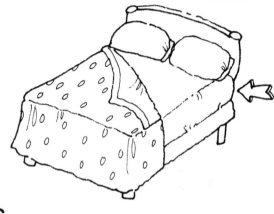

It's __ __ __ __ __

3. It starts like **sl**eep ends like tr**im**.

It's __ __ __ __

4. It starts like **gr**ound and ends like t**apes**.

It's __ __ __ __ __ __

1. Use the underlined letters to make new words.

2. Color the picture that shows **someone** doing something.

1. <u>ch</u>in → _ _ _ _ _  ←sm<u>art</u>

2. <u>dr</u>ip → _ _ _ _ _  ←s<u>ink</u>

3. <u>fr</u>ee → _ _ _ _ _  ←t<u>ame</u>

4. <u>pr</u>etty → _ _ _ _ _  ←s<u>ize</u>

1. Use the underlined letters to make new words.

2. Color the picture that shows a way to travel.

1. <u>st</u>are → _ _ _ _ _ 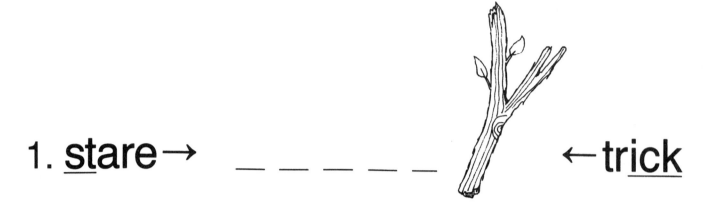 ←tr<u>ick</u>

2. <u>sh</u>are → _ _ _ _  ←tr<u>ip</u>

3. <u>tr</u>ick → _ _ _ _ ←cl<u>ap</u>

4. <u>wr</u>ite → _ _ _ _ _  ←sl<u>ap</u>

1. Use the underlined letters to make new words.

2. Draw a picture for each word you make.

1. <u>fl</u>at   _ _ _ _ _ _   sh<u>ow</u>er

2. <u>t</u>ake   _ _ _ _ _   <u>able</u>

3. <u>sn</u>ack   _ _ _ _ _   sh<u>ak</u>e

4. <u>st</u>and   _ _ _ _ _   sh<u>ore</u>

1. Use the underlined letters to make new words.

2. Put the new words in order to make a sentence.

1. <u>l</u>ip   _ _ _ _   s<u>o</u>ng

2. <u>dr</u>ip   _ _ _ _ _   st<u>ove</u>

3. <u>be</u>fore   _ _ _ _ _ _   ou<u>tside</u>

4. <u>br</u>ing   _ _ _ _ _ _   r<u>idge</u>

John _ _ _ _ _   _ _ _ _ _ _

the _ _ _ _ _   _ _ _ _ _ _ .

Look at the picture (symbol) for each letter in the secret code. Write the letter for each picture on the lines below.

A = ◐   E = ▨   G = ◮   I = ◯

M = ▢   R = △   T = ▱

What are you?

I __ __ __ __ __ __ __ __ __!

1. Use the code to find out what to do.

2. Do what it tells you to do.

A =L   D = ⌐   G = ⊓•

O =L•   R = \   W = /

⌐ \ L /   L   ⌐ L• ⊓•

1. Decode the secret message.

2. Follow the directions in the message.

A = L   B = ◺   E = ◣   F = ⌐

G = Γ   K = ⌐   L = ◢   M = □   U = ■

— — — — — —
□ L ⌐ ◣ L

— — — —
◺ ◢ ■ ◣

— — — — .
⌐ ◢ L Γ

This is called the "Letter Before" code. Can you guess why?

B = A   F = E   I = H   T = S

U = T   X = W   Z = Y

__ __ __ __

U I B U

__ __ __

X B T

__ __ __ __ .

F B T Z

Finish the code by writing the letter that comes before the letter shown.

B = C   C = D   = E   J = K

= M   = O   = R R = S   = T

How can you send a secret message?

_   A   _   _   A   _   _   _   _   _   _
L   J   D   R   D   B   Q   D   S

_   _   _   _ .
B   N   C   D

61

This is the "Game" code. Match the letters with their game symbols.

= C = E = I = M

= N = O = P = R

= S = T

How can your team win?

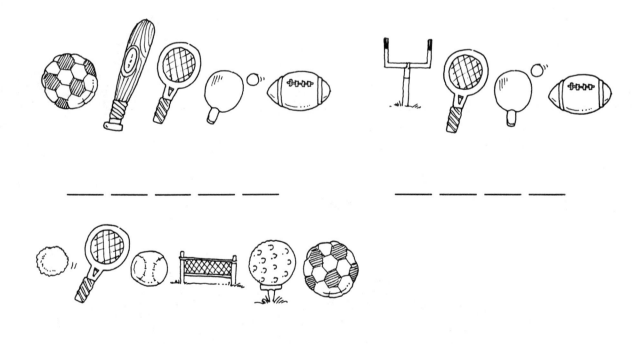

__ __ __ __ __   __ __ __ __

__ __ __ __ __ __ __ .

This is the "Letter After" code.

D = E   E = F   K = L   N = O

Q = R   R = S   S = T

What comes in the mail?

K N S R   N E
‾ ‾ ‾ ‾   ‾ ‾
K D S S D Q R
‾ ‾ ‾ ‾ ‾ ‾ ‾ .

This is the "Funny Animal" code.

A =    E = 🐕   H = 🦁

O = 🐥🐥   T = 🐟   Z = 🐔

Where should you use this code?

__ __   __ __ __   __ __ __ .

Finish making the "Letter Before" code by writing the ABCs in order in the boxes.

B = A   C = B   D = C   E = ☐

F = ☐   G = ☐   H = ☐   I = ☐

J = ☐   K = ☐   L = ☐   M = ☐

N = ☐   O = ☐   P = ☐   Q = ☐

R = ☐   S = ☐   T = ☐   U = ☐

V = ☐   W = ☐   X = ☐   Y = ☐

Z = ☐

___ ___ ___ ___ ___
J   L O P X

___ ___ ___   ___ ___ ___ ___.
U I F   B C D T

1. Use the code from page 65 to write a message to your friend.

2. See if your friend can read the message.

Find the letter that is missing from each group of words. Fill in the letters to solve the riddle at the bottom of the page. The first one is done for you.

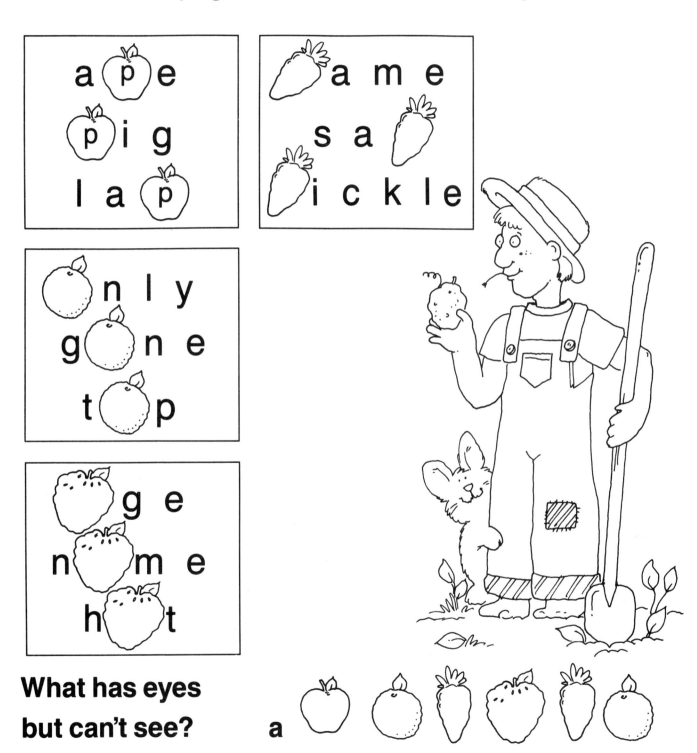

a (p) e

(p) i g

l a (p)

___ a m e

s a ___

___ i c k l e

___ n l y

g ___ n e

t ___ p

___ g e

n ___ m e

h ___ t

What has eyes but can't see?

a

Find the letter that is missing from each group of words. Fill in the letters to solve the riddle at the bottom of the page.

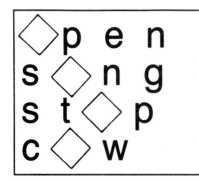

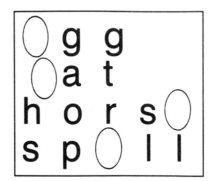

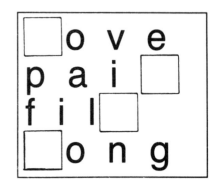

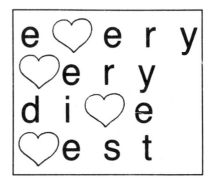

What has fingers but can't use them?

Find the letter that is missing from each group of words. Fill in the letters to solve the riddle at the bottom of the page.

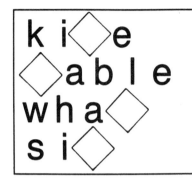

k i ◇ e
◇ a b l e
w h a ◇
s i ◇

b ♥ n e
♥ v e r
s p ♡ t
m ♡ t h e r

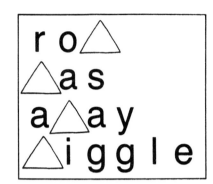

r o △
△ a s
a △ a y
△ i g g l e

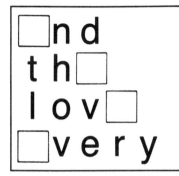

☐ n d
t h ☐
l o v ☐
☐ v e r y

◯ a z y
t a l ◯
p ◯ a y
◯ u c k

What gets wet when it's drying?

a ◇ ♥ △ ☐ ◯

1. Start at the bottom.

2. Climb the ladder by changing one letter on each rung. Use the letters from the box.

```
i   p   d
```

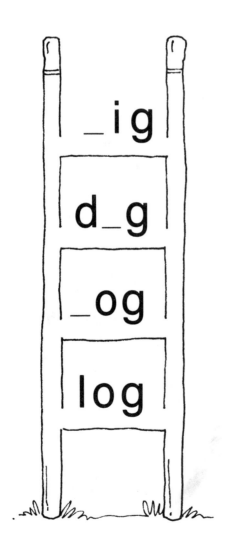

_ig

d_g

_og

log

Use the letters from the box to help you make new words as you climb the ladder.

n   c   o

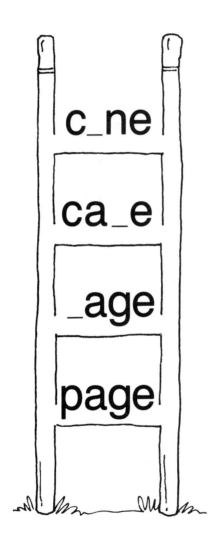

c_ne

ca_e

_age

page

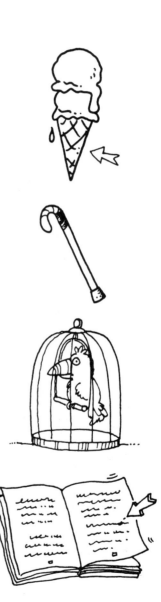

Use the letters from the box to help you make new words as you climb the ladder.

p	s	c

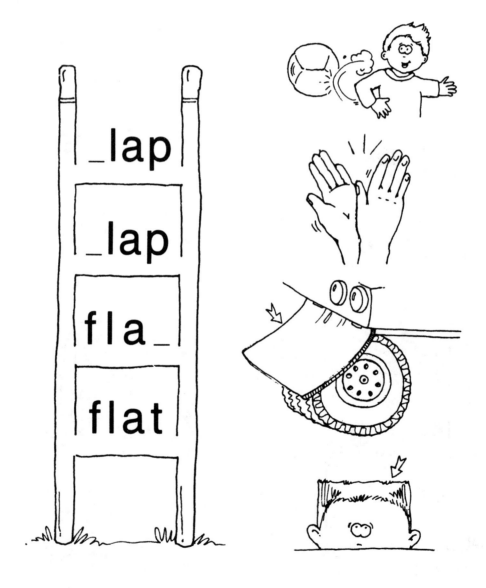

_lap

_lap

fla_

flat

Use the letters from the box to help you make new words as you climb the ladder.

s g m

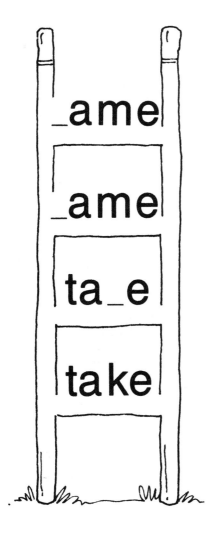

_ame

_ame

ta_e

take

1. Change the vowel to make a new word.

2. You may use any vowel that makes a word:
   a, e, i, o, and **u** are vowels you may use.

1. wit   w _ t

2. had   h _ d

3. bat   b _ t

4. sit   s _ t   or   s _ t

A Silly Square has words that can be read down or across.

Example:

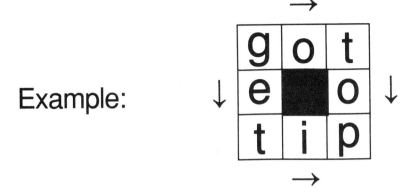

Use a vowel to make a new Silly Square.

The vowels are **a, e, i, o, u,** and sometimes **y.**

1. Write the vowels __, __, __, __, __, and sometimes y.

2. Use the vowels to make a Silly Square.

1. Consonants are all the letters that are not vowels. Cross out the vowels below and you will have the consonants.

a b c d e f g h i j
k l m n o p q r s t
u v w x y z

2. Make a Silly Square. Write a consonant in each blank square.

b	e	a	
o			e
a			a
	o	a	

1. Write the missing consonants: b c _ f _ _ j k
   _ _ n p _ r s _ v w _ y _ .

2. Use some of the consonants to finish the
   Silly Square.

Try this Silly Square with only two pictures to help you.

	o	a	
r			o
i			o
	a	i	

1. Make a Silly Square of your own.

2. Draw some pictures to go with your square.

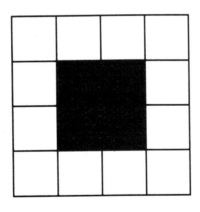

Palindromes are words that are the same when you read them left to right or right to left.

Here are some palindromes:

gag   pop

Fill in the missing letters to make more palindromes.

Try each vowel **(a, e, i, o,** or **u)** until you make a word.

b _ b   d _ d   m _ m

These palindromes need 2 letters. Try vowel pairs **(aa, ee, ii, oo,** or **uu)** to complete these words.

p _ _ p   t _ _ t   n _ _ n

Many names are palindromes.

Try to write these palindrome names.

N _ _   B _ _   E _ _

These people are standing in alphabetical order.

Copy their names on the lines.

_____   _____   _____

Here are some longer palindromes. The middle letter will be different when a palindrome has <u>5</u> letters.

Example: RADAR

1. Draw a red circle around each R.

2. Draw a blue circle around each A.

Can you use the same pattern to make these palindromes?

k a __ __ __

m a __ __ __

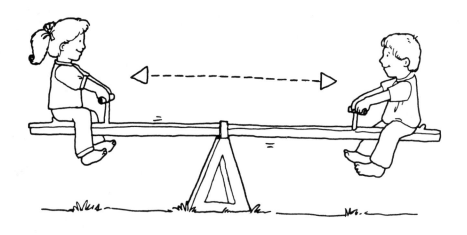

l e __ __ __

Some words spell new words when written backwards.

Example: **pin** backwards spells **nip**

1. Write these words backwards.

2. Draw a line from your new word to its picture.

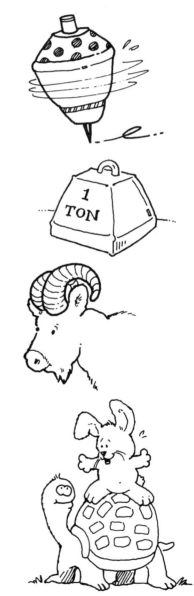

not _ _ _

no _ _

pot _ _ _

mar _ _ _

Anagrams are words whose letters are mixed up.
Unscramble these letters to make words.
Draw a line from your new word to its picture.

atb   __ __ __

yob   __ __ __

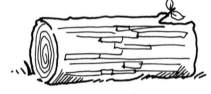

ogd   __ __ __

ogl   __ __ __

atr   __ __ __

Unscramble these anagrams to make words. Use the letters to solve the riddle at the bottom of the page.

geg = △ g g __

rgil = __ __ __ ◇

nkig = __ ○ __ __

clema = □ __ __ __ __

What did the penguin ride to work?

an ○ □ ○ □ ◇ △

Unscramble these anagrams to make words. Use the letters to solve the riddle at the bottom of the page.

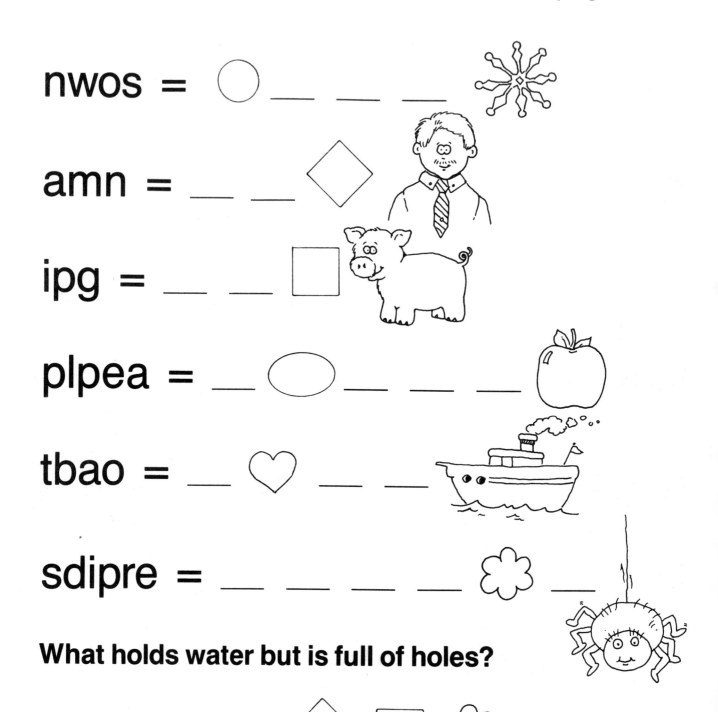

nwos = ◯ __ __ __

amn = __ __ ◇

ipg = __ __ ▢

plpea = __ ⬭ __ __ __

tbao = __ ♡ __ __

sdipre = __ __ __ __ ✿ __

What holds water but is full of holes?

a ◯ ⬭ ♡ ◇ ▢ ✿

Unscramble these anagrams to make words. Use the letters to solve the riddle at the bottom of the page.

eirf = __ __ __ □

anir = ◇ __ __ __

dnha = __ ⋈ __ __

aktbse = __ __ △ __ __ □

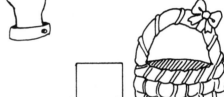

gthin = __ ○ __ __ __

lcuod = ◯ __ __ __ __

What goes up but never moves?

a △ □ ⋈ ○ ◇ ⬭ ⋈ △ ▭

Move the letters in the underlined word around to make a new word.

Make **taco** into something you wear. ___ ___ ___ ___

Make **slid** into something to cover jars. ___ ___ ___ ___

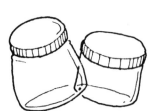

Change **mean** into what we call someone. ___ ___ ___ ___

Make **near** into a way to get money. ___ ___ ___ ___

1. Read the clues.

2. Write the answers for the across clues going across → like GO.

3. Write the answers for the down clues ↓ like B
   E.

4. Let the pictures help you.

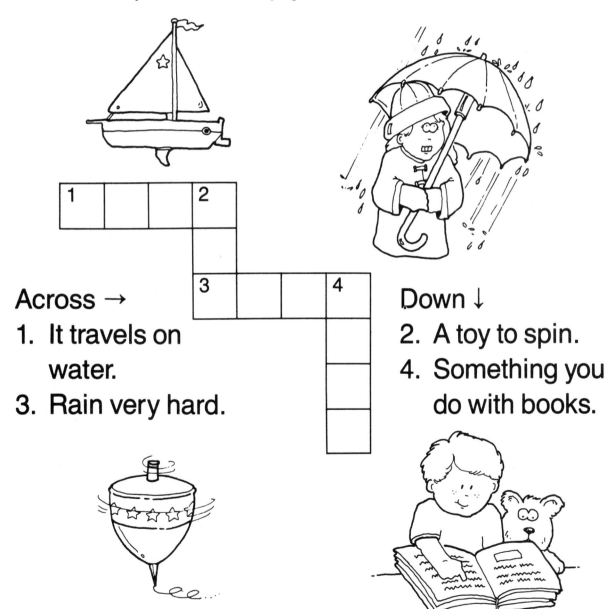

Across →

1. It travels on water.
3. Rain very hard.

Down ↓

2. A toy to spin.
4. Something you do with books.

1. Read the clues.
2. Write the answers.

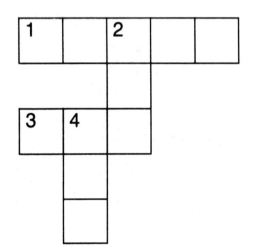

Across →
1. A place to sit and eat.
3. You do it to food.

Down ↓
2. A Halloween animal.
4. A large jungle animal.

1. Read the clues.

2. Write the answers.

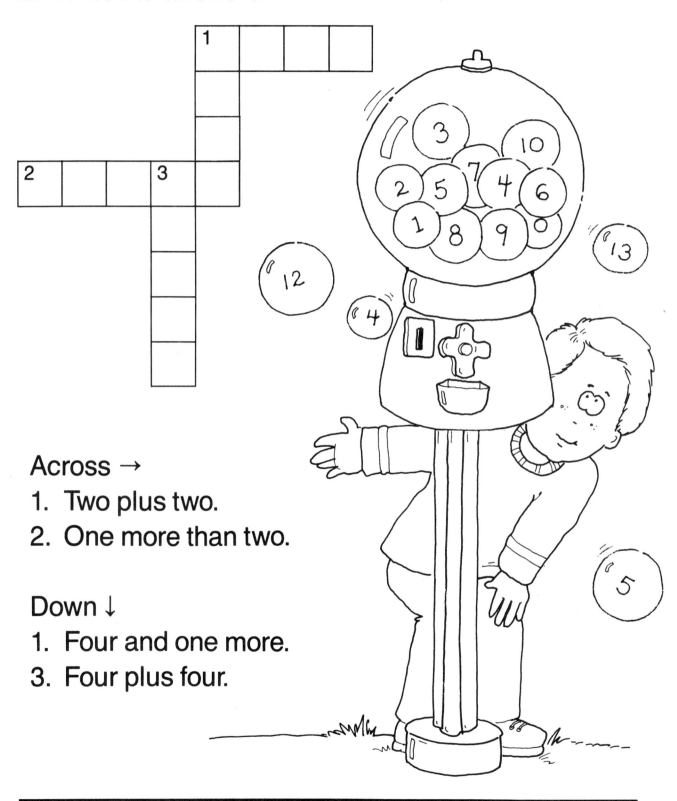

Across →

1. Two plus two.

2. One more than two.

Down ↓

1. Four and one more.

3. Four plus four.

Opposites are words that mean very different things.

Write the opposites. Fill in the letters to solve the riddle at the bottom of the page.

Up and **down** are opposites. **Sit** and **stand** are opposites.

The opposite of **go** is ___ ⋁ ___ ⊔

The opposite of **big** is ___ ___ ___ ___ ___ ◯

The opposite of **near** is ___ ___ △

The opposite of **play** is ___ ___ ___ ✿

The opposite of **night** is ___ ___ ▭

The opposite of **take** is ___ ☁ ___ ___

What do you call a cat who just washed her hair?

a ▢ △ ◯ ◇ ◇ ▭

✿ ☁ ◇ ◇ ▭

Finish each line with a word that rhymes with the underlined word.

The little **<u>cat</u>** had on a __ __ __ .

There was a **<u>tear</u>** in the baby __ __ __ __ .

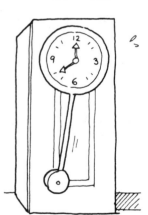

The huge **<u>clock</u>** said tick __ __ __ __ .

She took the **<u>car</u>** out of the __ __ __ .

Page 7

4	3	8
9	5	1
2	7	6

Page 8
Answers will vary.

Page 9

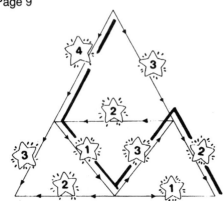

Page 10
yellow kettle — 3 + 4 + 1

7 2 (3) 1 6
4 3 (4) 2 5
5 6 (1) 0 5
7 3 4 1 4

red kettle — 1 + 3 + 4 + 2

1 2 5 4
5 6 2 1
(1 3 4 2)
8 0 5 4

orange kettle — 4 + 3 + 5

6 1 2 8
3 7 3 5
6 7 0 3
(4 3 5) 8

Page 11
Answers will vary.

Page 12
Answers will vary.

Page 13

10 = H − 3 − 5 − 7 − C
14 = H − 3 − 5 − 6 − C
19 = H − 3 − 7 − 2 − 2 − 5 − C
22 = H − 3 − 5 − 7 − 2 − 5 − C

Page 14
Missing numbers — 18, 7
Numbers used more than once — 17, 5, 8
Number greater than 20 — 35

Page 15	over	up
robot	1	1
stuffed bear	5	5
skates	2	6
soccer ball	4	4
fire truck	3	5
pony	1	3
blocks	4	1

Page 16
1. Casey, 332
2. Samantha, 387
3. Jon, 222
4. Benjie, 279
5. Michael, 249
6. Adam, 264
7. Marta, 178
8. Erica, 321

Page 17

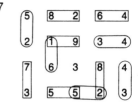

Page 18
Answers will vary.

Page 19
1 + 6 = 7
9 − 5 = 4
5 + 4 = 9
7 − 2 = 5
6 + 2 = 8
5 − 3 = 2
4 + 4 = 8
6 + 6 = 12

Page 20
Top road = 6
Middle road = 4
Bottom road = 8

Page 21

Page 26
6 + 5 + 0 + = 11
7 + 3 + 2 = 12
8 + 4 + 1 = 13

Page 28
Greatest — 6
Answers will vary.
Least — 4
Answers will vary.

Page 29

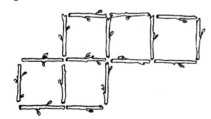

Page 30
1) 6 1 8
2)

Page 31

1.

2.

3.

Page 32

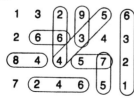

Page 33

1	3	2	9	5	6
2	6	6	3	4	3
8	4	4	5	7	2
7	2	4	6		5	1

Page 35
48¢

Page 36

Page 40

1.)

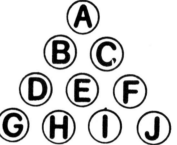

2.)

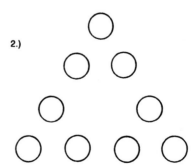

95

Answers

Page 41

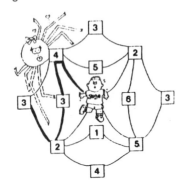

Page 42
14 squares
8 triangles

Page 43
5 + 4 = 9   3 + 2 + 2 + 2 = 9
4 + 2 + 2 = 8   7 + 1 = 8
3 + 3 + 3 = 9   3 + 2 + 3 = 8
10 − 3 = 7   2 + 5 = 7
3 + 3 + 1 = 7

Page 44
```
      2
  5   8   6
  3   1   4
      7
```

Page 46

Page 47

Page 49
MILK AND QUACKERS

Page 50
cat, game, bag

Page 51
swing, green, chain

Page 52
bright, sheet, slim, grapes

Page 53
chart, drink, frame, prize

Page 54
stick, ship, trap, wrap

Page 55
flower, table, snake, store

Page 56
long, drove, beside, bridge
John drove beside the long bridge.

Page 57
I AM GREAT!

Page 58
DRAW A DOG.

Page 59
MAKE A BLUE FLAG.

Page 60
THAT WAS EASY.

Page 61
MAKE A SECRET CODE.

Page 62
SCORE MORE POINTS.

Page 63
LOTS OF LETTERS.

Page 64
AT THE ZOO.

Page 65
I KNOW THE ABCS.

Page 66
Answers will vary.

Page 67
potato

Page 68
glove

Page 69
towel

Page 70
log, dog, dig, pig

Page 71
page, cage, cane, cone

Page 72
flat, flap, clap, slap

Page 73
take, tame, game, same

Page 74
wet, hid, bit, set or sat

Page 75
try, yet, pet, tap

Page 76
pig, gag, tag, pot

Page 77
bear, read, toad, boat

Page 78
boat, tied, need, bean

Page 79
goat, tool, pail, grip

Page 80
bib, dad, mom, peep, toot, noon

Page 81
BOB, EVE, NAN

Page 82
kayak, madam, level

Page 83
ton, on, top, ram

Page 84
bat, boy, dog, log, rat

Page 85
egg, girl, king, camel, icicle

Page 86
snow, man, pig, apple, boat, spider, sponge

Page 87
fire, rain, hand, basket, night, cloud, staircase

Page 88
coat, lids, name, earn

Page 89
Across 1. BOAT 3. POUR
Down 2. TOP 4. READ

Page 90
Across 1. TABLE 3. EAT
Down 2. BAT 4. APE

Page 91
Across 1. FOUR 2. THREE
Down 1. FIVE 3. EIGHT

Page 92
stop, little, far, work, day, give, pretty kitty

Page 93
hat, bear, tock, jar